First published in Great Britain in 1996 by Brockhampton Press,
a member of the Hodder Headline Group,
20 Bloomsbury Street, London WC1B 3QA.

This series of little gift books was made by Frances Banfield,
Kate Brown, Laurel Clark, Penny Clarke, Clive Collins, Melanie
Cumming, Nick Diggory, Deborah Gill, David Goodman, Douglas
Hall, Maureen Hill, Nick Hutchison, John Hybert, Kate Hybert,
Douglas Ingram, Simon London, Patrick McCreeth, Morse Modaberi,
Tara Neill, Anne Newman, Grant Oliver, Michelle Rogers,
Nigel Soper, Karen Sullivan and Nick Wells.

Compilation and selection copyright
© 1996 Brockhampton Press.

ISBN 0 86019 461 3
A copy of the CIP data is available from the
British Library upon request.

Produced for Brockhampton Press by Flame Tree Publishing,
a part of The Foundry Creative Media Company Limited,
The Long House, Antrobus Road, Chiswick W4 5HY.

Printed and bound in Italy by L.E.G.O. Spa.

The Funny Book of RUGBY

Words selected by
Bob Hale

Cartoons by
DOUGLAS INGRAM.

BROCKHAMPTON
PRESS

And Dusty Hare kicked 19 of the 17 points ...
David Coleman

No friends, Rugby is for watching - not playing.
*Spike Milligan, **Scunthorpe Revisited,***
Added Articles and Instant Relatives

After the game, having covered themselves
with mud and glory, rugger players spend hours
and hours in the bath, and then expect you to
talk to other rugger wives while they put down
pint after pint of beer. Occasionally in the back
of a car, they will make a forward pass at you.
*Jilly Cooper, **Men and Super Men***

Rugby: a game played by men
with funny-shaped balls.
Anonymous

Coarse Rugby is played by those who are too old, too young, too light, too heavy, too weak, too lazy, too slow, too cowardly or too unfit for ordinary rugger.

Michael Green, **The Art of Coarse Rugby**

He's like a needle in a haystack, this man - he's everywhere!

Ray French

Although he amazed the spectators with his pace and sidestepping abilities, Basil Maclear failed to make an impact on the English rugby selectors. They disapproved of his individuality (he used to wear white gloves on the pitch). However, Ireland had no reservations in picking him and he made his debut in 1905. In the three matches he played against England he scored tries in two.

The Guinness Book of Sporting Blunders

'Rugby is a game for the mentally defective,'
he agreed.
'That is why it was invented by the British. Who
else but an Englishman could invent an oval ball?'
Peter Pook, **Pook's Love Nest**

I've taken a lot of stick. The lads are calling me
'Lurpak' – the best butter in the world.
Steve Hampson

In 1884, Wales half-back Harry Gwynn dashed
through Scotland's defence but failed to touch
down for a try - he was cheekily looking for
someone to pass to. Sadly, he took too long
and Scotland's defenders tackled him.
Gwynn lost the ball and Scotland the match.
The Guinness Book of Sporting Blunders

Rugby Song: **If I were the marrying kind**
If I were the marrying kind,
Which I thank the Lord I'm not, Sir
The kind of man that I would wed
Would be a rugby full-back.

And he'd find touch and I'd find touch,
We'd both touch together,
We'd be all right in the middle of the night
Finding touch together.

If I were the marrying kind,
Which I thank the Lord I'm not, Sir
The kind of man that I would wed
Would be a wing three-quarter.

And he'd go hard and I'd go hard,
We'd both go hard together,
We'd be all right in the middle of the night
Going hard together.

If I were the marrying kind,
Which I thank the Lord I'm not, Sir
The kind of man that I would wed
Would be a centre three-quarter.

And he'd pass it out and I'd pass it out,
We'd both pass it out together,
We'd be all right in the middle of the night
Passing it out together.

If I were the marrying kind,
Which I thank the Lord I'm not, Sir
The kind of man that I would wed
Would be a rugby fly-half.

And he'd whip it out and I'd whip it out,
We'd both whip it out together,
We'd be all right in the middle of the night
Whipping it out together.

If I were the marrying kind,
Which I thank the Lord I'm not, Sir
The kind of man that I would wed
Would be a rugby scrum-half.

And he'd put it in and I'd put it in,
We'd both put it in together,
We'd be all right in the middle of the night
Putting it in together.

If I were the marrying kind,
Which I thank the Lord I'm not, Sir
The kind of man that I would wed
Would be a rugby hooker.

And he'd strike hard and I'd strike hard,
We'd both strike hard together,
We'd be all right in the middle of the night
Striking hard together.

If I were the marrying kind,
Which I thank the Lord I'm not, Sir
The kind of man that I would wed
Would be a big prop-forward.

And he'd bind tight and I'd bind tight,
We'd both bind tight together,
We'd be all right in the middle of the night
Binding tight together.

If I were the marrying kind,
Which I thank the Lord I'm not, Sir
The kind of man that I would wed
Would be a referee.

And he'd blow hard and I'd blow hard,
We'd both blow hard together,
We'd be all right in the middle of the night
Blowing hard together.

In 1896 E.F. Fookes had a chance to save an
England match against Ireland. Unfortunately,
enthusiasm got the better of him - he got the
ball ran over the try line and ... kept on running
straight into the dead ball area. Ireland went
on to secure a 10-4 victory.
The Guinness Book of Sporting Blunders

The tradition is in safe hands.
I wish I could say as much for the ball.
Michael Green, **The Art of Coarse Rugby**

When a rugby player yelled as his dislocated
shoulder received attention, the nurse pointed
out that a woman had just given birth to a baby,
with much less fuss. 'Maybe,' said the player, 'but
let's see what happens if you try to put it back.'
Stuart Turner, **The Public Speaker's Bible**

In 1897 the Scottish rugby union were so confident of retaining the Calcutta Cup they didn't even bother bringing it to the match with them. England won 12-3.

The Guinness Book of Sporting Blunders

A boy came home from his first rugby match with a broken nose, a torn ear and three loose teeth, but he couldn't remember who they belonged to.

Traditional rugby joke

In 1971 the All Blacks lost their first-ever series to the British Lions. Matters weren't helped during the Third Test when Howard Joseph tripped over a boxer dog whilst on a try-scoring run. He never played an international for his country again - what became of the dog's rugby career is not recorded.

The Guinness Book of Sporting Blunders

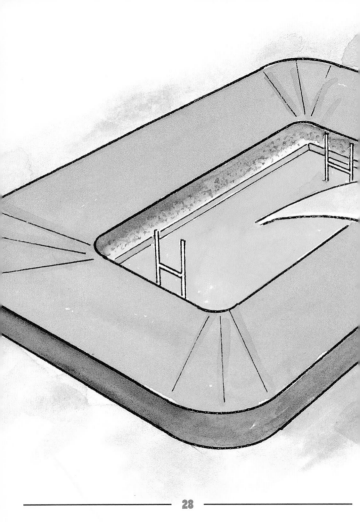

To most rugby players, fitness is for getting
to the bar first, and tactics is for getting
someone else to pay for their round.

Leo and Jilly Cooper

If you ask me, once rugby players have succeeded
in getting their boots on the right feet, the
mental challenge of the game is largely over.

Derek Robinson's wife, in **Run with the Ball**

When the England rugby captain Fred Stokes
saw the state of the West of Scotland pitch before
the 1873 international the night before the match
he arranged to have metal bars fitted to the soles
of his team's boots. Sadly, it made little difference
and the result was a scoreless draw.

The Guinness Book of Sporting Blunders

In my time I've had my knee put out, broken my collar-bone, had my nose smashed, a rib broken, lost a few teeth, and ricked my ankle, but as soon as I get a bit of bad luck I'm going to quit the game.

J.W. Robinson

Henry Taylor lost the chance for his England cap in 1881 when he arrived at the wrong railway station and the team left without him.

The Guinness Book of Sporting Blunders

It is always useful to have a first-aid expert on the team. Not to heal the injured, but to order the removal of hurt opponents, whether they need it or not.

Michael Green, **The Art of Coarse Rugby**

Sport is absurd, and sad.
Those grown men, just look,
In those dreary long blue shorts,
Those ringed stockings, Edwardian,
Baldi pates, and huge
Fat knees that ought to be heroes.
James Kirkup, **Rugby League Game**

After a match in 1986 Wally Lewis, the former
Australian rugby league captain, was given a clean
bill of health. He was quite surprised, especially as
he had replaced his urine sample with flat lager.
The Guinness Book of Sporting Blunders

The Wigan defence allowed
him two bites at the shot.
Radio Manchester reporter

That could have made it 10-3, and there's a
subtle difference between that and 7-3.

Bill Maclaren

At one end of the scale are giants with thighs like
oak trees, who break three ribs, have them roughly
strapped up, and return to run eighty yards and
score the winning try. At the other end are pimply
adolescents feebly chasing each other in a barren
meadow at the end of the Piccadilly Line. The
same laws apply to both of them.

Michael Green, **The Art of Coarse Rugby**

Dolway Walkington goes down in rugby history
as one of the game's earliest eccentrics. The
cavalier player is reported to have taken to the field
wearing his monocle which he carefully removed
before he made tackles.

'I don't know what you see in rugby,' my wife said.
'It's always the same – a lot of hyperthyroids
dashing about in their underwear.'
Derek Robinson, **Run with the Ball**

It seems a neat game,
but do they really bite ears off?
Elizabeth Taylor

In my first year, 1834, running with the ball to
get a try was not absolutely forbidden, but a
jury of Rugby boys of that day would almost
certainly have found a verdict of 'justifiable
homicide' if a boy had been killed in running in.
Thomas Hughes

Hal Sever was probably the best winger in English rugby union during the 30s. However, few will forget his last international in 1937/8 when he dramatically ran into a goal post losing not only the ball but his teeth as well.

The Guinness Book of Sporting Blunders

Then there was the case of the player who damaged a finger. As the first-aid case was in its usual ransacked condition, they splinted it with a teaspoon and his laces and sent him off to hospital.

'What's the matter?' asked a medical student.

'I can't move my finger,' replied the player.

'No wonder,' said the student, 'you've got a damn great teaspoon tied to it.'

Derek Robinson, **Run with the Ball**

With ungirt loins I face the foe,
Their clutching hands elude.
I hear not all the players' cries,
Their honest voices rude.

My feet scarce touch the muddy earth
As o'er the sward I fly.
The line is 'neath my pounding boots,
I dive - I've scored a try.

And thus it is in life itself,
In life as in Rugby's game.
Ungird your loins, my boy, and strive
For the goal of an honest name.

Anonymous

In 1974 during the British Lions tour of South Africa both the Springboks' scrum-halves were injured so the South African team replaced them with one Gerrie Sonnekus - a player who normally played No. 8. Not only did he play brilliantly he even scored a try.

Sean Edwards has happy memories of Wembley. On his last appearance here he fractured his cheekbone.

Ray French, on Great Britain's Rugby League captain

Arnold Alcock will be remembered as the only misprint ever to play for England. He was capped against the Springboks in 1906 much to the surprise of everyone - especially Lancelot Slocock who should have been on the team list.

The Guinness Book of Sporting Blunders

One of the greatest international cliffhangers took place at Twickenham in 1914 when England and Scotland incredibly fielded 11 new caps between them. England won 10-9 in the last eight minutes thanks to a Willie Watts fumble. He never played for his country again.

The Guinness Book of Sporting Blunders

Roses are red, violets are blue.
St Helens 21, Wigan 2.

Telegram sent by St Helens' Alex Murphy when his team beat Wigan in the 1966 Rugby League Challenge Cup final

In Scotland, Rugby is the game of the Classes; the masses are devoted to Association, with the exception of one district generally classed as the Borders where Rugby is the game of the populace.

Badminton Library on Football, 1899

In 1913 Ronnie Poulton (later Poulton-Palmer) was the dashing hero of English rugby at the beginning of the century. It was both the country and the game's loss when he was shot by a sniper during World War I.

The Guinness Book of Sporting Blunders

This stone commemorates the exploit of William
Webb Ellis, who with a fine disregard for the rules
of football as played in his time, first took the ball
in his arms and ran with it thus originating the
distinctive feature of the Rugby Game. AD 1823.

Plaque on the wall of the Close at Rugby School,
unveiled in 1923

All matches are drawn after five days or after
three days if no goal has been kicked.
The Laws of Football As Played At Rugby School, 1846

Patrick Esteve's determination to place the
ball directly under the posts, thus helping
his kicker, proved a costly mistake for France
when they played England in 1985. To the
delight of the Twickenham crowd scrum-half
Richard Harding refused to give up the cause
and continued pursuing the French player
after he had crossed the try-line. His
perseverance paid off when he caught up with
the Frenchman, knocked the ball out of
Esteve's hands and helped England to a 9-9
draw. France missed the Grand Slam by
a single point.
The Guinness Book of Sporting Blunders

Soccer is a contact sport -
rugby is a collision sport.

Anonymous

Recent market research data has shown a high
correlation between the profiles of beer drinkers
and rugby enthusiasts.

Chris Zanetti, Allied Beer Brands

J.E. Junor was picked to play for England against
Scotland in 1881 but the game was postponed twice.
Unfortunately, he had to leave for India before the
game was rescheduled - he never won his cap.

The Guinness Book of Sporting Blunders

What I find myself doing is reflecting on the rewards of comradeship a simple game gave a lad who was growing up. As boys we were told that sport is about the friends you will make and now I am an old guy I realize how true that was.

Jackie Kyle

Going on tour can destroy some people with its emotional pressures, so, in selection, you are looking at character as well as ability.

Ian McGeechan

During the 1924 rugby league Challenge Cup final a mounted policeman got in the way of Wigan's Adrian Van Heerden. The South African winner sidestepped the English horse and scored a try. Wigan won.

The Guinness Book of Sporting Blunders

Acknowledgements:

The Publishers wish to thank everyone who gave permission to reproduce the quotes in this book. Every effort has been made to contact the copyright holders, but in the event that an oversight has occurred, the publishers would be delighted to rectify any omissions in future editions of this book. *Classic Sports Quotes*, Peter Ball and Phil Shaw, Chancellor Press; *5000 One- and Two-Line Jokes*, Leopold Fechtner, Thorson's; *The Huge Joke Book*, Goldstein, Jackson, Ford and Newman, Random House Inc.; *Murphy's Law*, Arthur Bloch, reprinted courtesy of Methuen, London; *And Finally ...*, Martyn Lewis, reprinted courtesy of Hutchinson, part of Random House; *The Random House Book of Jokes and Anecdotes*, Joe Claro, reprinted courtesy of Random House Inc.; *Just Say a Few Words*, Bob Monkhouse, reprinted courtesy of Arrow Books, part of Random House UK Ltd.; *The Guinness Book of Sporting Blunders*, Guinness Publishing Company Limited; *The Art of Coarse Rugby*, Michael Green, reprinted courtesy of Richard Scott Simon Agency; *Run with the Ball,* Derek Robinson; *Rugby Songs and Ditties*, Scott Milway and Jamie Macleod-Johnstone, published by WCP.